CACTI

CACTI

MATTHEW SWEENEY

Secker & Warburg
POETRY

First published in Great Britain 1992
by Martin Secker & Warburg Limited
Michelin House, 81 Fulham Road, London SW3 6RB

A CIP catalogue record for this book
is available from the British Library

ISBN 0 436 50842 7

Set in 10/12½ Bembo
Printed in Great Britain by
St. Edmundsbury Press Ltd, Bury St. Edmunds

FOR BILL SWAINSON

CONTENTS

ACKNOWLEDGEMENTS

Acknowledgements are due to the following:

Arvon Anthology 1989, BBC Radio 4, *Bête Noir*, *High on the Walls: a Morden Tower Anthology*, *Irish Studies Review*, *Irish Times*, *London Magazine*, *Observer*, *The Orange Dove of Fiji*, *Pivot*, *Poetry Book Society Anthologies 1989*, *1990* and *1992*, *Poetry Book Society Bulletin*, *Poetry London Newsletter*, *Poetry Review*, *The Printer's Devil*, *Robert Greacen: A Tribute at 70*, *Sage Eye*, *Sunday Times*, *Times Literary Supplement*, *Verse*

'The Aviary' won a prize in the 1989 Arvon Poetry Competition.

'Cacti' first appeared in *Poetry*.

'Give Him Coffee' uses lines and phrases from the writings of Lorca, and details from accounts of his life.

The author acknowledges assistance from the Arts Council of Great Britain, and from the Authors' Foundation and the K. Blundell Trust.

SUGAR

From the high window he watches
his father's light plane
clear the mountain
and head for the rising sun.
He lies back on his bed
and thinks of sugar,
and the toffee he'll make
when his father gets back.
Next door he hears his mother
is up and dressed, and knows
she'll be in, opening curtains,
warning of breakfast,
and soon the smells of coffee
will drift upstairs
under his door,
coffee without sugar.
He imagines a line of ants
night after night
crossing the veranda,
each with a grain in its jaws.
He imagines keeping bees,
their sweetening hum
filling the garden
as he approaches
in his white armour.
He goes again to the window
where the usual gunfire
crackles beyond the river.

TORCHLIGHT

Listen, the squeak of sandals on parquet floor,
the swish of a monk's brown habit . . .
It's Bob again, Bob of the biceps, Bob
who'll heave boys out of bed and slap them,
in the sudden daze of torchlight,
and make a date for the morning.

Whispers down the dorm link Bob
with the young nun in the sick bay,
the one I stare at, go there to see.
Soon she'll leave, I know that –
I half know why. It's there in
The Italian Girl I read under the bedclothes.

It's there, or I force it there,
then lie in the dark, thinking,
while whispers precede an ambush,
perhaps for me, that'll mean squeals
and scuffles, and the prefect's arrival
with his torch-beam bouncing off the floor.

SINGING

Singing never pleased his grandma.
It sent her up the appletree
to howl, and she was big,
a danger to the bottom branch.
What was it about singing
that bugged her? Her ears
could cope with shouting, easy,
but put a tune in there,
sit it on the surest voice,
and she'd be out, and up the tree.
The cat used to stare at her.
The grandson rattled coins
and contemplated genes.
He quizzed her about affairs
with tenors, in the 20s.
He took up the guitar,
wrote bad songs, and practised
in the disused toilet
at the top of the garden.
His voice attracted gulls.
He did the odd shit while up there,
for old times' sake. On days
when the wind was from the North
shreds of his songs reached the kitchen
and his pot-stirring grandma.
He'd have to coax her down
while the stew burned.

THE AUNT I NEVER MET

The aunt I never met was black-haired
and holy. She sang in the choir
on Sundays. She also helped
my grandfather butcher the lambs
he kept in the long grass at the back –
even he agreed she was the best
with the cleaver. She played tennis
with priests, and beat them,
and drank Bloody Marys from a bottle
during whist drives, and owned
the only yellow bubblecar in Ulster
(now in a private collection
in Guersney). During the war
she took up German, crossed her sevens,
lit the odd bonfire at night
on the cliff edge, and did no good.
French toast and salmon were her favourites.
She hated kids – her eventual undoing,
if you ask me. Why else did she
end her days in that old farmhouse
hidden by trees, where the outside light
stayed on all night to lure
visitors, even family, who never came?
Why else did I never meet her?

BIG FRANK

Often in the dregs of daylight
he'd be on the course,
or if not, he'd want me to be –
his travelling partner,
his teenage accomplice, or worse.
Lights on, he'd come to check me.
Knowing my silhouette,
he'd leave the engine running
and, chuckling accompaniment,
'Nocturnal walloper', he'd shout.
Weekends, we'd do the rounds
of the county's courses –
we'd lurk in the car
till he saw a likely pair
approach the clubhouse.
Straight away he'd challenge them
for a fiver a head.
'Me and the boy', he'd say
in his suspect way.
'We'll take you on. How's that?'
Out on the tee he'd whisper:
'Drop your club when they hit.
Cough when they putt.
They won't expect any better,
they know you're a kid.'
But I was too arrogant
for that, I *knew* we would win.
I could swing the club
(in this I was wrong)
and I wasn't playing alone.
And he had all the style –
birdies, from well off the green.

Lying on his mouth and nose
to line up the putt,
then rattling it in,
under the turned-up toe
and the grimace; the grunt
to match my cheer
as I ran to claim the ball,
savouring the affront
to likeliness. He had his éclats
in his singular way,
and I was his sidekick,
his fifteen-year-old straight man,
and no one could say
we didn't try to lick them,
didn't very often win
on the 18th green –
or in open competition,
as the last pair in.

THE HILL

After the visitors and their children,
after the rearlights have vanished,
I go inside to stare out at the hill
that fills my window, and I remember
climbing there with a Christian Brother –
I must have been ten – and sitting
by the cairn on top for an hour or more,
speaking little, watching the toy cars
move between villages, and the birds –
we had a dog with us, a black cocker,
who barked them away – come hovering close,
and I should have gone back there
when the house was full of shouts
and simmerings, but it's quiet now
in every room, and I go upstairs
to stare out at the sea instead, past
a flurry of starlings, heading somewhere.

HERE

Under a grey, dry sky
a muted light comes off the sea,
and children with skateboards and a football
play beneath my window
where I sit at a desk and stare
past the finches on the wire,
happy to let seconds evaporate
till days, a month, are over.

No running along the wrong platform
among the sheets and poles of renovation;
no waiting, with a beer, for the plane –
those were days back, might be years,
so completely am I here,
but so fully was I there, too,
that I will be again.

There in the city of roof-gardens
overlooked by blocks,
of pubs with nooks and fizz-free ale,
of heaving, blanking-out crowds –
and here, with hedges and a sea
with no boats on it, no vapour-trails
in a sky that fuzzes hills
but will let the stars poke through.

A gull laughed at me,
laughed three times and flew on,
and the smell of dried blood
rose from the green
and followed me on the wind.
There was no escape
in the sandstone, no caves
to hide in, and the sea
was stormy, the beach boat-free.
I caught a magpie
with the side of my eye, heading
towards the house
where a family of swifts
sat on the wires
outside my window, and saw
right through me
day after day, and the baby
flew in once, and turned
in the trapped air
above me, then flew back out.
Why would it stay there?

THE EAGLE

My father is writing in Irish.
The English language, with all its facts
will not do. It is too modern.
It is good for plane-crashes, for unemployment,
but not for the unexplained return
of the eagle to Donegal.

He describes the settled pair
in their eyrie on the not-so-high mountain.
He uses an archaic Irish
to describe what used to be, what is again,
though hunters are reluctant
to agree on what will be.

He's coined a new word
for vigilantes who keep a camera watch
on the foothills. He joins them
when he's not writing, and when he is.
He writes about giant eggs,
about a whole new strain.

He brings in folklore
and folk-prophecy. He brings in the date
when the last golden eagle
was glimpsed there. The research is new
and dodgy, but the praise
is as old as the eagle.

OWENIE, LATE

Late-riser among the medicine bottles –
antacid, tagamite – your white head
flashes in the mirror, red face beneath,
and (sleeping downstairs now) you shuffle
out to the kitchen table, where a scone
half-survives, where a knife's in the jam,
and the teapot's already being filled.

Too soon for smiling, for speaking even,
you hear banter from the wireless
as Lad, the collie, watches from the doorway,
and you half-watch the road
that slides past the bottom of the garden
on its way to the sea you swam in
but know now you'll never drown in.

HIS DOG

Where is this dog he sees and I can't?
Why is he pointing to the window,
then beckoning me to rise from bed
and herd his sheep back to the hills?
All around me sick men sleep through
his hissed commands, his tearing cries
that the night-nurse runs to calm —

a calm that night-lights can't prolong,
or daylight either, though his daughters
when they come with wills that lack
his signature, don't get a sound
or a move from him, don't get the farm,
although they plead and squabble.
Where is his dog now, where is it?

A PECULIAR SUICIDE

Begin with the note left on the table,
saying 'You'll never find me',
in a ring of photographs of sons.

Ask the moustached, diving policeman
how many river-holes he searched
where the salmon spawn in glaur.

Ask his colleagues, ask the long one
who searched the farm – he'll tell you
he found nothing bar the note.

Ask the neighbour who played dominoes,
as usual, with him in the bar
the night before he disappeared,

and who saw the spade was missing
from its usual place, and got
the assembled police wondering why.

Got them scouring the grassland
around the house, until finally
they found it, and freshly laid sods

hiding planks and a bin-lid
with a rope attached, and a tunnel
that didn't go very far.

Ask what they found at the end –
just him, and the pill jar,
and the coldest hot-water bottle of all.

THE CAVE

Inside the cave
was where he stayed
all winter,
emerging only to
prise mussels
from the rocks
at low tide,
check his lines
or rabbit traps,
shoo off strangers.
Old army coats
and driftwood fires
kept him warm
enough to live,
to write daily
in a notebook
in a cramped script
he never read.
Still, the pages
filled, and pen
succeeded pen,
till one Spring day
when rain slanted,
he poked a stop,
dropped the pen
and walked out
with the notebook,
crossed the beach,
climbed the road
to a telephone,
dialled, and waited
till a woman's voice

flew round his head
and out again,
into the notebook
where it stayed.

WHATEVER

What does he think, this man
in the hospital bed, knowing
he's dying because he heard
she was sleeping with a neighbour –
perhaps she taunted him
until he grabbed the bottle
of weedkiller, and swallowed,
and now his kidneys are dead,
dead as he'll be soon?

And what does she think, knowing
she called in the other man
who, showing it was harmless,
swallowed weedkiller too –
and he's in another hospital,
fighting to live, and the whole
town is talking about her
and her two kids, and all
because of sex, love or whatever?

BISCUIT MEN

Making biscuits shaped like men,
baking them until they're brown,
eating all the heads, and then . . .
He always got stuck here, as though
he was one of the biscuit men,
and the cardboard woman he imagined
singing the nursery rhyme
in the piny kitchen   was standing
by his elbow in the study
where he went every day to try
to get past these rhymes,
to bleed them out of his head.

But they wouldn't go, and she
was down on the street again,
beneath his window, bags at her feet,
while a cabbie braked,
then reached up to switch off
his yellow light, as she got in
without a glance up at him
where he'd stand for hours.
. . . dumping them into the bin . . .
Dumping one . . . He still had a head
that was full of nursery rhymes
or bits, and she was their star.

CACTI

After she left he bought another cactus
just like the one she'd bought him
in the airport in Marrakesh. He had to hunt
through London, and then, in Camden,
among hordes of hand-holding kids
who clog the market, he found it,
bought it, and brought it home to hers.
Next week he was back for another,
then another. He was coaxed into trying
different breeds, bright ones flashing red –
like the smile of the shop-girl
he hadn't noticed. He bought a rug, too,
sand-coloured, for the living-room,
and spent a weekend repainting
the walls beige, the ceiling pale blue.
He had the worn, black suite re-upholstered
in tan, and took to lying on the sofa
in a brown djellaba, with the cacti all around,
and Arab music on. If she should come back,
he thought, she might feel at home.

CORKS

After he'd thrown the first cork
at his own reflection, he knew
he'd flipped, especially when
he kept on raining corks
at that foxy beard
and the darker hair above it
(what was left) and the length
of face in-between.
He was accurate, too –
all those dinner parties
just as the guests were leaving –
so accurate he winced
when the corks met glass.
The left eye hurt most.
The corks bounced to the ground
to be picked up and re-thrown,
and once, for verity,
he uncorked a Chardonnay,
took one swig as he freed
the cork from its screw,
sniffed it, and threw it
so hard his nose hurt
and went on hurting,
so he lay on the bed
and thought of all she'd said
till his nose throbbed in sleep.

HIS DREAMS

He dreamed he was found on the sofa
saturated with his own blood.
He dreamed his daughter picked her nose
as she walked behind the coffin.
He dreamed the date of his death
and re-dreamed it the next night.
He ran to his homoeopathic doctor.

He took his pills and drops to bed
and didn't dream the first night.
Or did he, was that mood a dream
half-forgotten? The night after
he dreamed his wife's head
sawn in half down the nose,
the profiles mouth to mouth, in a kiss.

HANGING

Hanging from the lamppost
he could see far —
cars parked to the street's end,
the few late-night walkers
most of whom ignored him
hanging there. He could hear
screams and running feet,
also quick shuffles away
and, eventually, the wah-wahs
that came with blue lights
that led in the dawn.
Then the lights in all the houses
went on, and dressing-gown
wearers gathered, killing yawns.
And flashbulbs exploded,
though he couldn't hold
his head up, and his face
was blue. A megaphone
asked the crowd to go home
as a ladder leant on the lamppost
for someone to ascend.
He looked into this man's eye
as the knife cut him down.

DIGGING

Out in the park two children are digging,
two girls, their long hair wind-tossed and free.
They are making little headway
although they lean with all their might.
Someone ought to tell them their flat shovel
is not the tool. Someone ought to take
that blown-off branch still sprouting leaves
that lies on the ground by their feet
and start a bonfire with it, let loose
its green smoke. Someone ought to say
it's too frail and long to plant,
too late to set. But the two girls keep digging,
with the mother-trunk firm above them,
and behind, the one lamp in the street still on.

SURPLUS LIGHT

Could be the making of your marriage,
or of your divorce. Try it at dusk,
when it comes into its own. Sit there
at my window with the curtains open,
as daylight shrinks behind silhouettes
of buildings like my own. See how
its headstart leaves the others standing
(which, of course, they are), even though
one hour later they're a staggered line
of lit streetlights on a night street.

Hard for you, I expect, to imagine
the effect on the nerves of witnessing
such relentless light, of seeing it
take on the sun and wear it down.
That's apart from its unlikely beauty –
my *iron star-tree* I could call it
but I won't. And to think that I rang
the Council to complain! What are rates
compared to this gift of surplus light,
this permanent reminder of wastage?

THE DESERT

He wanted *rim-bel-terfass* and nothing else.
He wanted a space-shot of the desert.
He wanted that Algerian woman he'd known
years before, who'd fed him *couscous*,
with rosewater made by her own mother.
He'd had a male friend who taught there,
on an oasis – he wanted him back there,
arriving, in the small hours, once a year
with dates, and goat-cheese, and the strong
red wines that held their own in France.
He wanted to be able to visit him –
take the train from Algiers, a rucksack
with bacon and whiskey on his back,
no advance warning, no Arabic, no French –
and send a series of postcards to himself
till, one by one, they all arrived back.

rim-bel-terfass: a stew made of gazelle meat, with Saharan
truffles (Sahara dish)

Larousse Gastronomique

ARTIFICIAL BLOOD

As the artificial blood that saved him
was Japanese, he went to live in Japan.
And of course he found the raw fish
the best for his patched-up heart.
The doctors were reassuring too,
even if they spoke a stretched English
and couldn't laugh. He kept in touch
with his golfer son – golf was played
throughout Japan; perhaps one day
his son would visit with saké . . .
Some nights he'd walk to a noodle bar
and point, then eat. He'd hurry
past the geisha parlours, and maybe
he'd stop at a phone, then stay outside
till he was too tired to remember
those walks on the Malvern Hills
he'd taken too seldom, too long ago
when his son was little, his wife alive,
before his heart operation,
before the white, thin artificial blood
entered his body and led him to Japan.

MELON DAYS

That autumn the newspapers were numbing.
Even the books he read kept him awake,
applying the written lives to his own,
trying on the deaths. And when friends called
with facts of the deaths of fathers
he had already decided that sporadic
melon days were needed, whole days
where he'd eat only melons, and keep
his vital sacs and tracts in shape.
So he brought bags to the nearby market
and filled them with melons, after pressing
for ripeness and sniffing for taste,
and as he waited to pay on that first day
he heard a fat man vow to lose weight
yet carry on eating a hamburger.
'Melon days', he muttered, 'That's what you need.
Melon weeks. Melon years.' But the girl
who gave him change stared at him
and shook her head as he walked away.

TRAVEL

for George Bowering

Is this what happens after travel,
this tickle in the throat,
this half-hearted coughing?
Alien viruses filtered through airports
breed quickest, it seems.
The duty-free whiskey is needed
because vitamins ran out.
Late nights with beers in a bath
full of ice-cubes, the company
of writers. How are *their* throats
at their various ends of the earth?
Who'll be the first to recover?
Someone I knew once would never
travel, said his body
wouldn't know the flu-germs
in the new place. He was right,
but think of the friendships avoided,
the stories over lunch
while hangovers faded, or were set up
in bars where the beer came
in jugs to your table
and the accents were varied.
The frisking of bookshops
for books not available
in the home-shops. The invitations
to share a hotel for a week
and risk wrecking your health.

BREACHES

for Irmgard Maassen

Glühwein with honey at Potsdamer Platz,
at the breach that drew the biggest cheer
when the pastel-coloured Trabis drove through.
Slush underfoot, wrecking shoes.
In the darkening distance: the Reichstag.

As we approached the Wall, we heard
a deepening tapping, a chipping that spread
till it was everywhere. Then we saw them:
men and women with mason's hammers and chisels,
and bags on the ground; two Frenchmen
attacking the parapet, making sure
nothing fell on the East; cracks that widened
to let blue-uniformed *Volkspolizei* peep through,
as they paused in their paired stroll,
while on the West, two cops in green
walked up and down, with megaphones,
advising the chippies to leave the Wall alone,
at once, or else . . . or else . . .

We took our tiny hammer and whacked chips
from that graffitti-daubed, astoundingly thin,
infamous construction, helping in our way
to make it disappear.

November 1989

THE OLD EASTERN
PROVINCES

He was telling me
about the old eastern provinces –
Silesia, Pomerania, East Prussia –
one night he'd broken out
his family heirlooms
of fine German wines,
wines I'd never dreamed of
and was loath to drink.
But drink we did,
and as we grew livelier
he brought out a map
of 30s Germany,
with Danzig, and Breslau,
and, of course, all Berlin.
We were in Baden,
next to Alsace –
which was German, he shouted,
as they all were
and would be again.

★

Twelve years later
I think of him.
I'm crossing Poland
by train – no zlotys,
not a Polish word,
only rusty German
which works with the old.
Eight parched hours
of flatlands and high-rises,
and horse-drawn ploughs.

In Wroclaw (Breslau)
someone will meet me
with zlotys and lead me
to my hotel –
but when the train brakes
in that cavernous station
I'm met by no one.

I lug my bag
through underground walkways,
out to the concourse
where the taxis wait.
I head inside
to Information,
past benches where old pairs,
out for the evening,
point and stare. A fat man
in a barber's chair
is shaved by a thin one.
The other shops are closed.
The queue at Information
is coiled round the room
and all the time Polish
is pouring from speakers,
giving me nothing –
until I hear my name.

In Karpacz (Krummhübel)
I practise my German
with old women in shops.
The accent is new to me
and soon to be extinct.

Up above, on Sněžka,
Czech borderguards
cradle their guns.
On the slopes is a ski-run,
and a ski-hotel
that once was a spa
for the German bourgeoisie,
and then, in the 30s,
a brothel. I sit there,
sip a beer, and think of him.

★

In six months I meet him
for the first time in years.
I'm in a restaurant
in Kreuzberg, and the Wall
is down. Soon there'll be
one Germany again,
and some will be looking east
and shouting over wine.
But he won't be one,
not this time, not to me.
We speak of the Black Forest
and remember student nights,
but not when he told me
about the old eastern provinces,
and I don't tell him
I've been to one.
I don't even think
we mention the Wall.

GIVE HIM COFFEE

('Give him coffee' was General Queipo de Llano's coded way of ordering his soldiers to shoot Lorca)

He was pain singing from behind a smile.
He was for gypsies, blacks and Jews.
He could drink brandy like no other,
and do without it for days. He heard
the wind blow over the heads of the dead,
the wind smelling of child's saliva, whooshing
through arches, searching for new landscapes,
new accents, newly created things.
He saw his own murder. Saw them
search the cafés, cemeteries and churches;
open barrels and cupboards; plunder
three skeletons to remove the gold teeth;
but never find him. Never find his body.
'Give him coffee, plenty of coffee',
the general had said, to soldiers
who did, and kept two bullets for his arse.

ONE HALF OF THE LOCAL POET SHOW

He motored up in his wheelchair
to address the puny audience.
He was one half of the local poet spot
before the boys on tour came on.
He was one angry, damaged man –
thalidomide?, something – and what
he read was angry and bad
but impossible to forget:
I want a thing with a hole in it.
My friend has a thing with a hole in it.
It cooks for him, it sleeps with him . . .
When he stopped, he left
and half the audience left with him,
so the big boys, 'Two of Ireland's best'
the poster said, stood up, one by one,
and read to a near-empty room.

NEW RULES

Even his dog ran with a limp,
following his lopsided run
along the path by the River Wye
where cyclists came up behind,
ringing their tinny bells, shouting
when the dog wouldn't limp aside,
and the man wouldn't either.

And you had to agree with them,
the lame dog and the lame man.
Even to get into a tracksuit lame
is admirable. But to go running,
or what passed for it, and to buy
a lame dog, or lame a good dog –
that's when you're talking new rules.

BLUE EGGS

The hens that laid the blue eggs
were Lavender Araucanas
and came from Chile, and the blue
(a darker blue than ducks' eggs)
got inside the shell as well,
and the eggs tasted better,
or so her friend said, proudly,
to people who'd never heard
of blue eggs, and who frisked
the friend for traces of a joke,
then finding none, asked
how they'd buy blue eggs,
how they'd contact her. But she
was on a farm somewhere, incognito
as any ex-teacher – and who
wouldn't be an *ex*-teacher
in these National Curriculum days
when they could box blue eggs.

BEARS

for Nicholas Jardine

Someone is sending me bears –
bear cards, teddybear cards,
I've had three so far.
'Apologies for bear militant'
introduced the last one,
and the bear was a German,
dressed as a sailor
in the First World War.
All the bears were German,
from the pensive first
through the pugnacious second
to the militant third.
And the handwriting is familiar
but forgotten – who is this
bear-man, or bear-woman,
and where will it end?
1920 is the latest date.
The soles of this bear's feet
are leather, and his eyes
are glass. His long nose
juts out over his collar.
The sewn-on red anchor
on his blue-serged arm
points to a paw in a cuff.
What will the next one wear?
When will enough be enough?

MONKEY

Even when the monkey died
they never invited us round
to eat green banana curry
and play braille scrabble
in that room underground
where twin hammocks hung
near the dead monkey's cage
that held him still, stuffed
and gutted, body-shampooed,
face locked in a rage
that quick death provides.
And none of us knew
what went on at the end,
whether poison, or heart,
or if one of them blew
their monkey away,
then turned on the other
and aimed that Luger,
that well-oiled Luger
at the brain of a brother,
but flung the gun down.
And with their excuse gone
we expected invites,
one big wake, perhaps,
complete with champagne,
and Joe, the taxidermist,
waiving his bill –
his grief-contribution,
his goody for the party.
We're all waiting still.

THE AVIARY

Isn't it wild that Mary
abandoned the aviary
and went to Jamaica?
Can't you see her there,
with birds nowhere,
only black boys?
Can't you hear the sea
and smell the coffee
overlaid with ganja?
Isn't that a buzzard
on the postcard
she's sending home?
Wasn't it five years
she spent with the birds
that bugged her?
Or was it the bars
and not the birds
she railed at?
All that wire
caging the air
for cameras.
All those feathers,
in all weathers,
to clean up.
Look at Mary now,
look at how
brown she's become.
Listen to her laugh,
isn't it rough
on the poor girl.
Imagine, she *flew*
from Heathrow

to be there.
Let's send Mary
a baby canary
with clipped wings.
Let's remind Mary
of the aviary,
let's wish her well.

THE BLIND MEN

They want it back, the blind men,
students of magnified touch,
evictees from this dingy house
whose bare walls they know by heart.
They want back in, and me out.
They still have keys they use
at night, to let me know –
by black hairs in the bath,
by a white stick under the stairs,
by tapping on bedroom doors
then not being there – that they
are the rightful tenants here,
and I've got to go. So I keep
the radio on, no television.
I stand in the mirrorless bathroom
and shave by touch, shivering
from the linoless floor. I cook
in the half-dark, and rarely work.
I keep my books hidden.
It's not as if it's a mansion –
the basement flooded last year,
as they will know, and the attic-
ladder's kaput – it's nowhere
to throw a party in, even if
people could find the street,
but they want it back, the blind men,
and they're not getting me out.

ASLEEP IN A CHAIR

Asleep in a chair for three hours?
Take that man away. Bind him
and bundle him into a mini-cab,
drive through the Southern English night
till you see the lights of Brighton,
then throw him out on the South Downs.

Hopefully it will be sub zero
and wet as Ireland. (*Drunk* and
asleep in a chair for three hours,
with the TV and the gas fire on?)
Pick a field with cattle in it,
or better still, a nervy horse.

Make sure there's no stream near,
or even a house. Get miles away
from a shop or a chemist –
empty out his pockets just in case.
Smash his glasses while you're at it.
Forget you liked him, lose his name.

Burn his shoes to ash beside him,
keep his jeans as a souvenir.
Cut his hair off (*all* his hair).
Asleep in a chair for three hours?
By the time you're finished, honey,
he might have learned to sleep in a bed.

THE DARK

There were owls in the moonlight
as we cleared the mountain –
such high fliers, such safe voles
in the fields underneath.
Then we swung out to sea
and back in, over the headland
with its ruined castle,
its football pitch, its cave.

Someone had kindly
lit bonfires on the touchlines,
but the pitch sloped
and the wheels threw up mud.
I managed to stop
in front of the goalposts,
and we took our sleeping-bag
to the dark of the cave.

BANKNOTES

A room empty except for banknotes
scattered on floorboards, and curtains
to keep this secret – and who
sent her the key and the address?
She had these four weeks before
she used them, begrudging the fare,
trudging through rain to a house
so dingy she tried to turn away.

But she'd travelled an hour, and the key
showed her the banknotes, like litter –
like leaves, as they were tenners
and inches deep. And watermarked, too,
in the torchlight. And when her bag
was bloated, she filled her clothes,
every item, then rustled to the door
she locked, holding onto the key.

THE SERGEANT

The sergeant blew the trumpet
to see what he could rouse,
then crouched in the dark
away from the bunkhouse.
After an empty minute
he rasped that note again,
and a third time, and fourth
till the yard was full of men.
Each was wearing trousers
and nothing else, and each
was squinting, searching
the dark for a face.
They'd kill, when they saw
where he was, but the lights
were dead, and there was no moon,
and the sergeant didn't twitch
when the women appeared
one by one, behind the men
who were muttering, and led them
back inside again,
leaving the sergeant
with his trumpet, outside
alone for a half hour
till he brought back the crowd.

AFTER CLOSING TIME

'Those who don't believe in life after death should be here after closing time': notice inside an office in Derry's city cemetery.

The gate will be open, and streetlights
will guide you through the graves,
but you'd better watch your carry-outs
as the dead are barred from pubs.
Watch for the flowers that fly
from grave to grave, creating letters
for the papers and maybe more dead –
and one thing you'll know in the half-light
is that the dead are too many
to fit in the ground, too lively
to lie in a box, so they do
what you'd expect them to, and that's why
they surround you as you swig
from a can. They ruffle your hair,
breathe through unbrushed teeth,
fart even, and one of the pushier
puts his finger in the hole in his head
then invites you to follow. Another
opens his rotting shirt to show you
his two hearts, the old and the new,
and a one-legged ex-pensioner
eyes the bulge of your cigarettes,
and you'd be well advised to drain
one can, then chuck the other
as far as you're able, for the dead
hate those who outlive them,
and you'd be canny to suss this
and run, and hope the gate's not shut.

DONEGAL, ARIZONA

for Dermot Seymour

He put Donegal in the oven,
cooked it awhile, and got Arizona.
And he siphoned all that rain
and the troublesome Atlantic
into waterholes in the desert
and the Colorado River.
A few tons of gelignite
moved the hills together
to make the Grand Canyon,
and he stretched all the toads
to make Gila monsters,
and bought a few steamboats,
and buried gold in the hills.
The Indians were difficult
but he advertised abroad,
then the Mexican ambassador
signed the Treaty of Guadalupe
all over again, and Derry
stared at Sligo over a void.